THE HISTORY OF THE SAN FRANCISCO 49ERS

Published by Creative Education
123 South Broad Street
Mankato, Minnesota 56001
Creative Education is an imprint of The Creative Company.

DESIGN AND PRODUCTION BY **EVANSDAY DESIGN**

LIBRARY OF CONGRESS CATALOGING-IN-PUBLICATION DATA

Bell, Lonnie.
The history of the San Francisco 49ers / by Lonnie Bell.
p. cm. — (NFL today)
Summary: Traces the history of the team from its beginnings through 2003.
ISBN 1-58341-313-8
1. San Francisco 49ers (Football team)—History—Juvenile literature.
[1. San Francisco 49ers (Football team)—History. 2. Football—History.] I. Title:
History of the San Francisco Forty-niners. II. Title. III. Series.

GV956.S3B45 2004
796.332'64'0979461—dc22   2003060473

First edition

9 8 7 6 5 4 3 2 1

COVER PHOTO: linebacker Julian Peterson

PHOTOGRAPHS BY
Corbis (AFP, Bettmann, Reuters), Getty Images, SportsChrome USA

CO 49ERS

Lonnie Bell

IN 1769, SPANISH EXPLORERS BECAME THE FIRST EUROPEANS TO SAIL UP THE CALIFORNIA COAST AND INTO SAN FRANCISCO BAY. SOON AFTER THAT, A SPANISH TOWN CALLED YERBA BUENA CROPPED UP ALONG THE BAY. IN THE MID-1800S, THE UNITED STATES RAISED ITS FLAG OVER THE TOWN AND CHANGED ITS NAME TO SAN FRANCISCO. TODAY, SAN FRAN CISCO IS A THRIVING PORT CITY AND POPULAR TOURIST DESTINATION KNOWN FOR ITS CABLE CARS, STEEP HILLS, AND GOLDEN GATE BRIDGE. THE CITY'S PROFESSIONAL FOOTBALL TEAM, THE 49ERS, IS ALSO SOMETHING OF A SAN FRANCISCO LANDMARK. THE FRANCHISE WAS FOUNDED AS PART OF THE ALL-AMERICA FOOTBALL CONFER ENCE (AAFC) IN 1946, BECOMING THE FIRST PRO FOOTBALL TEAM LOCATED WEST OF THE ROCKY MOUNTAINS. THE 49ERS—NAMED AFTER THE MINERS WHO CAME TO CALIFORNIA DURING THE GREAT GOLD RUSH OF 1849—JOINED THE NATIONAL FOOTBALL LEAGUE (NFL) IN 1950 AND HAVE BEEN ENTERTAINING BAY AREA SPORTS

[Running back Ken Willard]

THE 49ERS' FOUR seasons as an AAFC team were memorable ones, as head coach Lawrence "Buck" Shaw and quarterback Frank Albert led the club to a combined 39–15–2 record and an appearance in the 1949 league championship game. After the AAFC folded and San Francisco was accepted into the NFL in 1950, the 49ers found the going tougher and dropped to 3–9.

From 1951 to 1954, though, San Francisco put together a winning record every year. The team featured a number of outstanding players during the '50s. The defense was led by tackle Leo Nomellini and Hardy Brown, a small but ferocious linebacker. The offense was directed by quarterback Y.A. Tittle, who made a habit of throwing "alley-oop" passes to athletic running back R.C. Owens. "It's the strangest thing I've ever seen on a football field," one reporter noted. "Owens, a former basketball star, would gauge Tittle's throw, jump as high as he needed to snag the pass, and come down in the end zone for a touchdown."

The 49ers of the early 1950s also featured two other star running backs: Hugh "the King" McElhenny and Joe "the Jet" Perry. In 1952, the versatile McElhenny was named the NFL Player of the Year. In 1953 and 1954, Perry became the first player in pro football history to rush for more than 1,000 yards in two straight seasons. San Francisco fans began calling Tittle, McElhenny, and Perry the "Million Dollar Backfield."

In 1957, a new offensive leader came to town: rookie John Brodie, who soon replaced Tittle as the 49ers' starting quarterback. In 1960, Brodie became part of pro football history when the 49ers introduced the shotgun formation. In this pass-oriented formation, the quarterback lined up a few yards behind the line of scrimmage, and the center jettisoned the ball into his waiting hands.

With Brodie and fellow quarterback Billy Kilmer sharing time directing the offense, and with tackle Charlie Krueger anchoring a stout defensive line, the 49ers were a respectable team in the first half of the 1960s. Unfortunately, an NFL championship remained only a dream, as the 49ers never seriously contended for the Western Division title.

IN 1968, A former NFL defensive back named Dick Nolan took over as the 49ers' new head coach. Coach Nolan liked the talent he saw in San Francisco. By then, the team had a potent offense led by Brodie and wide receiver Gene Washington. On the other side of the ball, linebacker Dave Wilcox and veteran cornerback Jimmy Johnson spearheaded a solid defense.

These players carried the 49ers up the standings. In 1970, San Francisco went 10–3–1, captured the National Football Conference (NFC) Western Division championship, and won a playoff game over the Minnesota Vikings. In 1971 and 1972, the team won two more division titles but again fell short of the Super Bowl, losing in the playoffs each year.

End Cedric Hardman (right) and linebacker Dave Wilcox (left) led a stout defense in the early '70s

After that, though, Bay area fans watched sadly as the team slipped back into mediocrity for the rest of the 1970s. Defensive tackle Cleveland Elam played some great games during these years, but it wasn't enough. When the club plummeted to 2–14 in 1978, former college coach Bill Walsh was brought in as head coach. Walsh knew he had his work cut out for him. "I'll be honest with you," he told reporters. "Turning this team around will be no easy matter. It's going to take time."

In 1979, the 49ers made a big move toward turning things around by selecting quarterback Joe Montana with the 82nd pick in the NFL Draft. During his college career at the University of Notre Dame, the 6-foot-2 and 195-pound quarterback had led the Fighting Irish to some amazing come-from-behind victories. Still, many coaches and scouts thought he was too small and slow for the NFL. But Walsh liked Montana's easy-going brand of leadership and inserted him into the starting lineup in 1980.

With Montana leading the way, the 49ers jumped to an improved 6–10 mark. Late in the season, they also made headlines by overcoming a 35–7 halftime deficit to the New Orleans Saints to win 38–35. Fans saw the comeback victory—the biggest in NFL history—as a sign that good things were around the corner.

THE TEAM OF THE '80s>

THE 1981 SEASON was a year of firsts for the 49ers. Behind such rising stars as wide receiver Dwight Clark and safety Ronnie Lott, the 49ers finished with the best record in the league (13–3) and won the NFC Western Division for the first time since 1972. In the playoffs, they beat the New York Giants and Dallas Cowboys to win the NFC championship and advance to their first Super Bowl. In the Super Bowl, they outlasted the Cincinnati Bengals 26–21 to bring home their first world championship.

That victory signaled the start of a 49ers dynasty. Before the end of the decade, San Francisco would win three more Super Bowls to become the undisputed "Team of the '80s." After topping Cincinnati for the championship in 1981, San Francisco beat the Miami Dolphins (38–16) in 1984, Cincinnati again (20–16) in 1988, and the Denver Broncos (55–10) in 1989.

With each additional championship, the legend of Joe Montana continued to grow. A near-perfect passer who seemed to have a sixth sense for finding the open receiver, Montana became known as "Joe Cool" because of his ability to stay calm in the most pressure-packed situations. During his 14-season career with the 49ers, he would be named the league's Most Valuable Player (MVP) four times. "He's the kingpin," said Lott, "the reason we've been able to maintain this."

Of course, Montana had a lot of help. Among the many talented players who helped make San Francisco the most dominant team of the '80s were Lott, running back Roger Craig, receivers Jerry Rice and John Taylor, and cornerback Don Griffin. "Sure we have some great individual players," said Rice, "but so do many other teams. What we have that is unique is a collective desire to be the best football team ever."

Rice himself was a fine example of that desire. Considered by many to be the greatest wide receiver in football history, Rice joined the team in 1985 and topped the 1,000-yard mark in 12 of his first 14 seasons. Before his 49ers career ended in 2000, the swift and sure-handed receiver would catch 1,281 passes, score 187 touchdowns, and post 19,247 receiving yards—all NFL records.

THE 49ERS FELL just short of the Super Bowl in 1990,

losing in the NFC championship game. Then, in 1991,

Montana injured his elbow and was out for the season; he

would soon be traded to the Kansas City Chiefs. Luckily,

the team had a talented backup quarterback waiting in

the wings: Steve Young.

San Francisco fans, accustomed to the brilliance of

Montana, were skeptical of their new quarterback at first.

But Young quickly won over both fans and teammates.

The scrappy left-hander proved that he was willing to

do whatever it took to win, including throwing blocks

and taking big hits. In 1992 and 1993, Young tossed a

combined 54 touchdown passes and led the 49ers to the

NFC championship game each year. Both times, how-

ever, the Dallas Cowboys kept them from going to the

Super Bowl.

Then, in 1994, the 49ers signed star cornerback Deion Sanders. The incredibly fast Sanders—who was nicknamed "Prime Time" because of his love of television media attention—made six interceptions that season, returned three of them for touchdowns, and was named the NFL's Defensive Player of the Year. With Rice having yet another big season and defensive tackle Dana Stubblefield leading a fierce pass rush, the 49ers went 13–3 and roared into the playoffs.

San Francisco finally ended its NFC title game jinx by beating the Cowboys 38–28. Two weeks later, the 49ers crushed the San Diego Chargers in the Super Bowl, 49–26. Young, who set a Super Bowl record with six touchdown passes in the game, felt like he had finally escaped from the shadow of Joe Montana. After the game, the jubilant quarterback exclaimed to reporters, "I've got a monkey off my back at last!"

THE 49ERS REMAINED a strong team in the seasons that followed, but they could not get back to the Super Bowl. In 1997, under new head coach Steve Mariucci, the team won 11 games in a row and finished 13–3. The offense continued to revolve around Young and Rice, but the team also featured such talented newcomers as running back Garrison Hearst and receiver Terrell Owens. These players carried the team back to the NFC championship game. Unfortunately, amid windy and rainy conditions, the 49ers fell 23–10 to the Green Bay Packers.

The 49ers made another valiant run in 1998, going 12–4 and meeting Green Bay again in the playoffs. After an exhausting battle, the 49ers found themselves trailing the Packers by four points with only three seconds left. But Young then snatched victory from the jaws of defeat by rifling a 25-yard touchdown strike to Owens for a thrilling 30–27 win. Unfortunately, the 49ers could not muster the same magic a week later, losing to the Atlanta Falcons.

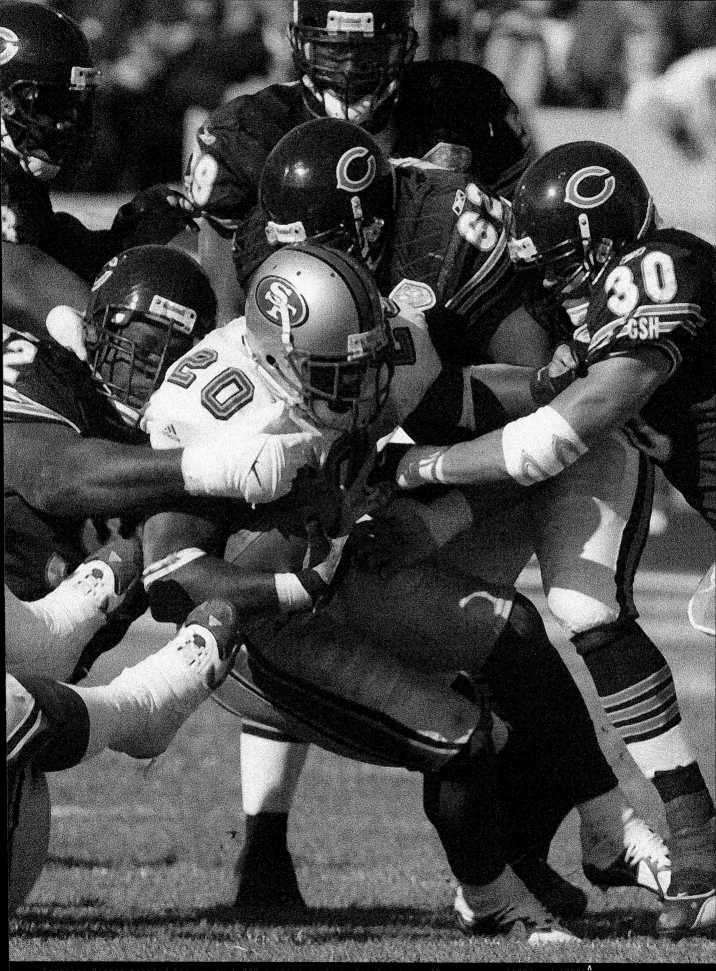

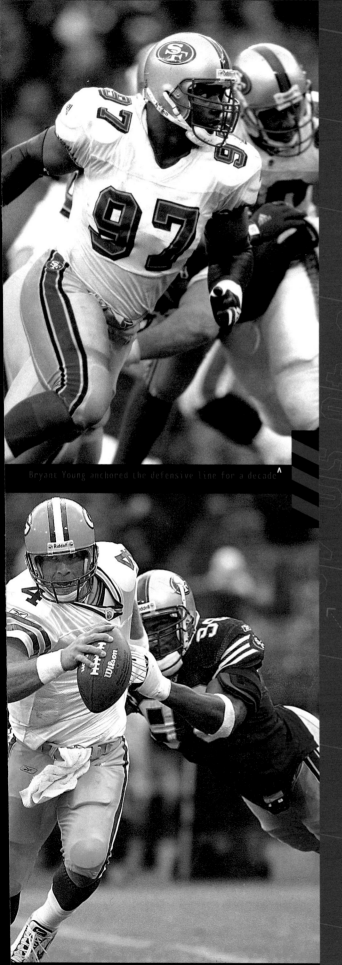

Bryant Young anchored the defensive line for a decade ^

Linebacker Andre Carter collected seven sacks in 2003 ^

In 1999, the 49ers suffered their first losing season (4–12) in 17 years. Young then retired and was replaced by Jeff Garcia. The small but quick Garcia proved to be a worthy successor by passing for a team-record 4,278 yards in 2000. Many of Garcia's passes went to Owens, whose great size (6-foot-3 and 230 pounds) and sure hands had made him one of the game's best receivers. In one game that season, Owens set a new NFL record with 20 receptions. "He's big, he can run, and if you play him one-on-one, he can outjump a defensive back," said St. Louis Rams defensive coordinator Lovie Smith. "He's the complete package."

Behind Garcia and Owens, the 49ers returned to the playoffs in 2001 and 2002. In the 2002 playoffs, San Francisco took on the New York Giants. The Giants opened up a 38–14 lead late in the third quarter, but the 49ers refused to give up. In the second-biggest comeback in NFL playoff history, San Francisco charged back to win 39–38, securing the victory with a Garcia touchdown pass with one minute remaining. It was a victory for the ages, and the red- and gold-clad fans in San Francisco's 3Com Park celebrated as if the team had just won a world championship.

Although the 49ers came up short of the Super Bowl in 2002 and 2003, fans in the Bay area remained as optimistic as ever. Garcia and Owens left town before the 2004 season, but such talented players as defensive tackle Bryant Young, defensive end Andre Carter, linebacker Julian Peterson, and running back Kevan Barlow promised to keep the 49ers near the top of the NFC West for years to come.

The San Francisco 49ers may have started out slowly, but they have since put together a record of success that is mind-boggling. Behind such legendary players as Joe Montana, Jerry Rice, and Ronnie Lott, the proud team in red and gold has won five Super Bowls and appeared in 10 NFC championship games since 1981. As today's 49ers carry on this tradition of excellence in one of America's most beautiful cities, this team by the Bay may soon strike gold again.

INDEX >